Clue Jr.®

The Case of the Winning Skateboard

Book created by Parker C. Hinter

Written by Della Rowland

Illustrated by Diamond Studio

Based on characters from the Parker Brothers game

A Creative Media Applications Production

SCHOLASTIC INC.
New York Toronto London Auckland Sydney

ISBN 0-590-13787-5

12 11 10 9 8 7 6 5 4 3 2 1   8 9/9 0 1 2 3/0

Printed in the U.S.A.   40

First Scholastic printing, February 1998

3 0646 00116 0922

Contents

1. The Case of the Glow-in-the-Dark
   Message   1
2. The Case of the Mud Puddle
   Mystery   11
3. The Case of the Mysterious E-Mail   23
4. The Case of the Backwards
   Birthday   35
5. The Case of the Locker Mess   42
6. The Case of the Doorbell Dodger   53
7. The Case of the Magazine Mix-up   62
8. The Case of the Winning
   Skateboard   73

Introduction

Meet the members of the new Clue Club. Samantha Scarlet, Peter Plum, Greta Green, and Mortimer Mustard.

These young detectives are all in the same fourth-grade class. The thing they have most in common, though, is their love of mysteries. They formed the Clue Club to talk about mystery books they have read, mystery TV shows and movies they like to watch, and also, to play their favorite game, Clue Jr.

These mystery fans are pretty sharp when it comes to solving real-life mysteries, too. They all use their wits and deductive skills to crack the cases in this book.

You can match *your* wits with this gang of junior detectives to solve the eight mysteries. Can you guess who did it? Check the solution that appears upside down after each story to see if you were right!

The Case of the Glow-in-the-Dark Message

The fourth grade science projects were due in a week. During lunch, Greta Green, Samantha Scarlet, and Peter Plum were discussing what they had made. But Mortimer Mustard didn't say a word. Finally Samantha asked him, "Are you going to tell us about your project, Mortimer?"

"I have to show you," said Mortimer. "Come over to my house this evening."

"Why can't we just come after school?" said Greta.

"Because it's better to see it when it's dark," said Mortimer mysteriously. "Let's meet in the clubhouse. That's where my project is."

"What is it?" asked Peter.

"You'll have to figure it out." Mortimer smiled. "But there will be clues for you."

That evening, Samantha and Greta showed up at the clubhouse after dinner. Peter was late, as usual. Finally, he came zooming up on his skateboard, with Bosco running behind him.

"Sit, Bosco!" Peter told his dog. "Sorry I'm late," he said to the others. "I had baseball practice." He dropped his baseball glove and cap on the floor and looked around the clubhouse in the dim evening light. "So where's Mortimer's project?"

"Don't know," said Greta. "All I see are a big box, a flashlight, and that piece of cardboard." She pointed to a flashlight and a piece of white posterboard on the table. On the floor next to the table was a large white box. A hole had been cut on one side of the box. There were two smaller holes above it.

Peter looked around the clubhouse.

Underneath the table was an open can of whitish paint. "I wonder if the paint is a clue," said Peter, looking into the can.

2

Bosco ran over to Peter and started sniffing the open paint can. When he did, he stepped on the lid, which was lying on the floor next to the can.

"Stop, Bosco!" Peter said. "I better put the lid on the paint or Bosco will knock it over."

"Maybe there's a clue inside the box," Samantha suggested.

Greta opened the top of the box and peered in. "I don't see anything," she told the others. One by one, they all looked inside. No one saw anything but an empty box. They looked around the clubhouse a while longer, but no one could figure out what Mortimer's mystery science project was.

"I guess we have to go to the house and get Mortimer," said Samantha.

"Yeah," said Greta. "I give up."

"Let's go," said Peter. He turned to his dog. "Stay, Bosco. Stay here, boy!"

Mortimer was busy helping his mom

3

with the dinner dishes when the kids came inside. "Hey, Mortimer," Samantha said. "Your science project is a mystery."

"Yeah," said Peter. "We can't figure it out."

"Come on," Mortimer laughed. "I'll show you." He hung up his dish towel and everyone headed back out to the clubhouse.

It was now dark outside. Mortimer picked up the flashlight and turned it on. "Maybe this clue will help," he said to the others. He aimed the flashlight at the piece of posterboard. When he turned the light off, the kids could clearly see glowing letters that read, *Shine the flashlight through the large hole in the box. Then look through the two small ones and turn the light off.*

"Wow!" exclaimed Peter. "Glow-in-the-dark paint!"

"Right," said Mortimer. "The sign was painted with glow-in-the-dark paint. The paint is white, so you can't really see it against the white poster or the inside of the box. When you shine a flashlight on it, then turn out all of the lights, you can see the paint in the dark. The glow fades out after a little while, so you have to shine the flashlight on it again."

"What's in the box?" asked Samantha.

"Another message," said Mortimer. "Follow the instructions on the sign." He pushed the flashlight into the bottom hole. "Who wants to look?"

"Me!" cried Greta. Mortimer switched off the flashlight and she pressed her face against the eye holes. "I see it! It says, 'This message was made with glow-in-the-dark paint.'"

"What a great idea, Mortimer," said Samantha after she'd looked into the box. "Your glow-in-the-dark project might win first place."

"Speaking of dark, turn on your flashlight, Mortimer," said Greta. "It's so dark in here. I can't see a thing."

"Sure," said Mortimer. He switched on the flashlight again.

Just then the kids heard a horn honk.

Peter looked out the clubhouse door and saw Bosco run to the driveway. "There's my mom," he said. "She's giving everyone a ride home." He looked around the clubhouse as the kids got ready to leave. "Anyone see my baseball glove?" he asked. The kids searched the clubhouse but the mitt wasn't there.

"Peter, you lose everything," Greta scolded.

"How could I lose my glove? We were here all the time," Peter said.

"No, wait! We went into the house to get Mortimer," said Samantha.

"I'll go tell my mom we'll be a few more minutes," Peter said, running to the car.

"Let's check inside, then," said Mortimer. But the mitt wasn't in the house, either. The kids sat down on the back-porch steps to think.

"Maybe your next-door neighbors took Peter's glove," Samantha said to Mortimer. "Remember when they 'borrowed' your ice skates without telling you?"

"They wouldn't take it," said Mortimer. "Besides, they're not home."

"Well, my glove couldn't just walk away," said Peter.

"Wait! Maybe it could," exclaimed Greta. "I think I know how to find the glove. I need your flashlight, Mortimer."

"Why?" asked Mortimer.

"We need it to see the other message," Greta replied.

"But I didn't leave another message," said Mortimer.

"I know," said Greta. "The glove snatcher did."

How does Greta know where to look for Peter's missing glove?

SOLUTION
The Case of the
Glow-in-the-Dark Message

Greta took the flashlight. Shining it in front of her, she led everyone back to the clubhouse.

"What does the message say?" asked Mortimer.

"This message isn't words," she told them. "It's tracks."

"Tracks? What tracks?" said Samantha, looking around.

"That's just it," said Greta. "No one can see them — yet!"

When they reached the clubhouse, Greta turned off the flashlight. On the ground were glowing paw prints. The kids started at the paint can and followed the prints out the door and around to the back of the clubhouse. Sure enough, there was Peter's baseball glove.

"I remember!" said Peter. "Bosco stepped on the paint can lid."

"It still had wet paint on it," said Mortimer. "So Bosco got paint on his paws."

"While we were in the house before, getting Mortimer, he must have carried the glove outside," said Samantha.

"Yeah. I saw Bosco's paw prints when we were looking for the glove in the clubhouse," said Greta. "Then Peter said his glove couldn't walk off, and I remembered the tracks again."

"Looks like you got the message, Greta," laughed Peter.

The Case of the Mud Puddle Mystery

Saturday morning Mortimer hopped out of bed and looked out his bedroom window. "Yuck! It's still raining," he sighed. It had been raining for two weeks. He sprinkled some fish food into his fish tank. "If it doesn't stop raining, you'll be able to swim outside your fishbowl," he told his goldfish, Jaws.

"I'm tired of all this rain," he told his mom at breakfast. "I can't do anything outside. At least I have the Clue Jr. Club meeting today. And everyone's coming over here, so I don't even have to go outside."

"Well, it rains a lot in April," said his mom, smiling. "You know, there's an old expression. 'April showers bring May flowers.'"

"Right," he answered glumly. "At this rate we'll have May flowers growing out of the sidewalks."

"Hmmm," said his mom. "That's a great idea for the poster contest at the art store. It's this afternoon. Did you forget?"

"Of course not," Mortimer replied. "After our meeting, we're going to make posters. We're supposed to come up with ways to keep the town clean and beautiful. The winner gets a free pass to the swimming pool for the whole summer!"

"I'll drive you to the art store after you're done," Mrs. Mustard said.

"Thanks, Mom! Today might not be so bad after all," said Mortimer.

During the Clue Jr. meeting, the kids decided to make one big poster together instead of one each. "That way, if we win, we'll all get free passes to the pool," Peter said.

"That would be so cool!" said Greta.

Mortimer came up with a slogan: "Keep Our Town Sparkling Like the Stars." The kids drew pictures of the town buildings with stars all around them. By the time they finished, the rain had stopped and the sun was shining brightly.

After lunch, everyone hopped into the car and Mrs. Mustard drove them downtown. She parked the car in front of the card shop, which was a couple of blocks from the art store. "I have to pick up some birthday cards," she told them. "Since it's not raining anymore, you kids can walk to the art store, okay?"

"That's fine, Mom," said Mortimer. "I'm happy to be outside now."

"Just watch out when you pass by the lot where they're building the new drugstore," said Mrs. Mustard. "The workers have dug up all the ground, so there are lots of mud puddles everywhere. Meet me back at the car at five. Have fun!"

The kids grabbed their rolled-up poster and took off down the street. As they got near the construction site, Richie Royal and Robbie Russet rode by on Robbie's bicycle. Richie was sitting on the seat and pedaling, while Robbie sat on the handlebars. When they saw the Clue kids, they screeched to a stop.

"Hey, Clue nerds, did you make a pretty poster?" Richie jeered. "Are you going to help clean up the city?"

"Yes," said Samantha. "Besides, the winner gets a free pool pass."

"Who cares?" sneered Robbie. "I'm not cleaning anything. And I don't need a free pass to the pool." He snickered.

"Yeah, you just jump over the back fence," said Greta.

"So what?" Robbie said. "Come on, Richie. Let's get out of here." Laughing, the boys rode off.

As the kids passed the building site, two girls came from the other direction. They were each carrying a poster.

"Look," said Samantha. "Here come Yolanda Yellow and Kitty Khaki. They made posters, too."

The girls waved at the Clue kids. Just

then, Robbie and Richie rode past Yolanda and Kitty. Richie swerved the bike in order to ride through a big puddle. Muddy water splashed all over Yolanda, Kitty, and their posters.

"Did you see that?" said Greta. "Richie and Robbie splashed mud on Yolanda and Kitty."

"Yeah, and they did it on purpose," said Peter.

The kids watched the two boys turn around and ride back toward the puddle. But before the boys could reach them, the girls ran up the block. Robbie and Richie splashed muddy water onto a car that was driving by instead. Some of the water went through the window, which was rolled down. The driver shouted at the boys, but they just sped off around the corner, laughing.

A few minutes later, Yolanda and Kitty came walking back down the street with Officer Lawford. "The boys were here just a minute ago," said Kitty.

"I don't see them now," said Officer Lawford.

"They rode through that mud puddle," said Yolanda, pointing to the large puddle. "They ruined our clothes *and* our posters."

The Clue Club kids overheard the conversation. "Should we tell Officer Lawford that we saw everything?" asked Samantha.

"Yes!" exclaimed Greta. "I can't stand to see Richie get away with anything."

The kids walked over to the group. Greta tapped Officer Lawford on his arm. "Excuse me," she said, "but we saw what happened."

"Yeah," said Mortimer. "Richie and Robbie splashed mud on Yolanda and Kitty — on purpose."

"Then they rode through the puddle again and splashed mud on a car," said Peter.

"Well, we'll wait here a few minutes and see if they come back," said Officer Lawford.

In a little while, Richie and Robbie came barreling around the corner, heading for the puddle again. When they saw Officer Lawford, they jumped the curb and rode down the sidewalk instead.

"You two," Lawford called out to the boys. "Come here a moment." Richie and Robbie skidded to a stop in front of Kitty and Yolanda, almost running into them.

"These girls tell me you deliberately splashed mud on them," Officer Lawford said.

"No way!" said Richie.

"You did, too," said Kitty. "Just a few minutes ago."

"You're crazy," said Robbie. "We've been in the park all morning."

"We saw you, too," said Greta. "You splashed the girls and a car."

"You Clue nerds are always poking your noses into someone else's business," snarled Richie. "And you're always trying to get me into trouble."

"Why don't you go find a real mystery to solve?" said Robbie.

"That's enough, boys," said Officer Lawford sternly. "I've got four witnesses who also saw you splash mud. What do you have to say now?"

"I say nobody can prove anything," said Richie. "It's our word against theirs."

"There!" said Yolanda. "See those bicycle tracks in the mud?" She pointed to muddy bike tracks coming out of the puddle. "Those are the tire tracks from their bicycle," said Yolanda. "That shows you they splashed us."

"Yes, I see," said Officer Lawford.

"How do you know those tracks are from our bike?" said Richie. "Anyone could have ridden through that puddle."

"Why don't you ride your bike through the puddle?" said Greta. "We'll see if the tracks are the same."

"That's a good idea," said Officer Lawford.

Robbie rode his bike through the puddle, beside the bicycle tracks that were already there. His tire tracks were not as deep as the others.

"I'm afraid these aren't quite the same tire tracks," said Officer Lawford.

"But how can that be?" exclaimed Kitty. "They splashed mud on us."

Officer Lawford shrugged. "There's nothing I can do."

"We're out of here," Richie said to Robbie.

"Wait!" cried Mortimer. "It is the same tire track. I can prove it!"

How can Mortimer prove the two tire tracks are the same?

SOLUTION
The Case of the Mud Puddle Mystery

"Do you need new glasses?" shouted Richie. "Look at the tire tracks."

"The tires are the same," said Mortimer. "It's the rider that's different . . . or rather, the *riders*."

"He's not making any sense," said Robbie.

"When you guys splashed the girls, you were both riding the bike," said Mortimer.

"I see!" cried Samantha. "Two riders are heavier than one, and that would make the tire track deeper."

"They should ride through the puddle again," said Greta. "This time together."

Sure enough, when both Robbie and Richie rode the bike through the puddle, the track was identical to the first one.

"I was thinking about stars on our poster," said Mortimer. "That's why I noticed the stars on the bike tires. Then I saw why the tracks were different."

"All right, boys," said Officer Lawford. "I'll give your parents a call. At the least, you should pay for cleaning the girls' clothes."

"Hey!" laughed Greta. "Looks like you guys are going to do some cleaning after all."

"Maybe they should help plant some flowers around town since they like to play in the mud," said Peter.

3

The Case of the Mysterious E-mail

On Monday morning, Ms. Redding announced that the fourth-grade class was starting a pen pal club. "We're going to exchange letters with a class of fourth graders in New Zealand," she told the kids.

Everyone in the class began talking excitedly. "Quiet down, class," Ms. Redding told them. "There's more. We're going to send our letters by E-mail. How many of you know what that is?" A few hands went up. Ms. Redding explained how E-mail works.

Greta raised her hand. "But I don't have a computer," she said. "How will I get E-mail?"

"Don't worry, we're going to use the school computers," said Ms. Redding. "In fact, part of your assignment in computer class will be to type up your letters and E-mail them."

"How do we get our mail?" asked one of the students.

"You'll have your own E-mail addresses," explained Ms. Redding. "The fifth and sixth graders here have been working with E-mail for a few months. Now we will be starting. Your E-mail address will be your first name and last initial plus our school's address. Here, I'll show you." She went to the blackboard, picked up a piece of chalk, and wrote *GretaG*. "For example, Greta, this is your E-mail address. Peter Plum's is *PeterP*. This way, it's easy for everyone to remember," Ms. Redding told them.

That morning, the children practiced sending each other E-mail in computer class. "After lunch, we're going to write letters to our pen pals," Ms. Redding told them. "So think about what you'd like to tell them about yourselves."

During lunch the kids discussed the new E-mail projects.

"Writing to a pen pal with E-mail will really be great," said Peter. "The messages will be here a lot quicker than by regular mail."

"I didn't get to send any E-mail today," said Greta. "We ran out of time before I was finished typing my letter. I hope I can figure out how to send an E-mail tomorrow."

"If you want, Greta, you can come over to my house after school, and I'll show you how it works," said Peter. "It's easy."

"Can't," she said. "I have karate class. By the way, I have a match Saturday afternoon. Can you guys come?"

"I'll be there," said Mortimer.

"Me, too," said Peter.

"Me, three," said Samantha.

"Oh, I almost forgot," said Greta excitedly. "Mr. Lee, my karate teacher, asked me if I could help out with some of the first-grade students. Well, actually I'm going to help Bart help the first graders."

"Bart who?" asked Peter.

"Bart Bronze," replied Greta. "You know, Betty's brother. He's sitting over there." She pointed to some older kids sitting at another table.

"Oh, yeah," said Samantha, rolling her eyes. "He thinks he's so cool."

"Well, he is good at karate," said Greta.

Just then Bart walked over to the table. "Hey," he said to Greta.

"Hi, Bart," said Greta.

"Mr. Lee says you're supposed to help me out on Saturday," Bart said.

"Yeah," said Greta.

"Well, just do exactly what I tell you to do, okay?" he told her.

"Sure," said Greta.

"I can't believe Mr. Lee asked a girl to help me," he muttered.

"What's his problem?" Mortimer whispered as Bart walked back to his table.

Brrriiiinnnnggg! "There's the bell," said Samantha. "Time to go back to class."

That afternoon, the fourth-grade class

worked on their letters to their pen pals.

After school, Greta waited on the playground for her mother to pick her up for karate class. The Clue kids discussed what they had written in their letters.

"I described all my fish," said Mortimer. "And all my favorite foods."

"I wrote about my birds," said Samantha. "Plus playing the violin."

"Did you tell your pen pal about helping in karate class?" Peter asked Greta.

"Of course!" said Greta. "I hope my pen pal is into sports." Just then, Greta's mother drove up. "There's Mom," she said. "See you tomorrow."

The next morning, Greta looked upset as she came running to meet the others on the playground. "Listen, guys," she panted. "Did I have my bookbag with me when I left school yesterday?"

"Yeah. I think so," said Peter, shrugging.

"Well, I can't find it," she said. "I didn't have it when I left karate, so I thought maybe I left it at school."

But when the kids went into school, they didn't find Greta's bookbag in her locker or their classroom.

"It's been stolen!" Greta wailed.

"Who would want to steal a bookbag?" asked Mortimer.

"You probably left it somewhere," said Samantha. "Someone will turn it in to the office. We'll go check after school."

That day in computer class, Greta had an E-mail message. It read: *Come to Mr. Lee's store at 4:30 to pick up something you lost.*

Greta showed the other kids her message. "It must be my bookbag," she told them. "But who knows I have an E-mail address?"

"Everyone in school knows about the E-mail," said Samantha.

"Yeah, maybe someone in your karate class saw your bag there, but they didn't think they'd see you today in school," said Mortimer.

"We'll go with you to pick it up," said Peter.

After school, the kids headed to Mr. Lee's School of Martial Arts. However, when they arrived, the karate store was closed and locked.

"Mr. Lee must be teaching a class," said Greta. "Sometimes he closes his store if he doesn't have anyone to work there."

"Maybe the person wanted to meet you in the back of the store," Samantha suggested.

The kids walked around to the back of the store.

Suddenly, Mr. Lee came to the back of the store with Officer Lawford.

"Greta!" exclaimed Mr. Lee. "What are you doing here?"

"I came to get my bookbag," Greta said.

"I just got a call telling me some kids were trying to break in," Officer Lawford told them.

"Not us, Mr. Lee," said Greta.

"Let's just take a look inside," said Officer Lawford. Mr. Lee unlocked the back door. "What's this?" said Officer Lawford.

He pointed to the floor behind the counter. There was Greta's bookbag with three sets of expensive karate uniforms inside, all her size.

The students who were practicing upstairs came down to see what was happening. Leading them was Bart. "Trying to get into the building to steal something, Greta?" Bart said.

"Someone left a message for me to come here," said Greta. "It said I would find something I lost."

"Who was that?" asked Officer Lawford.

"Well, I don't know," said Greta.

"That's a pretty wild story, young lady," said Officer Lawford.

"Yeah. Who's going to believe that?" said Bart. "Especially when her bookbag is full of loot."

"That *is* my bookbag, but it disappeared yesterday," said Greta.

"Sure," said Bart. "You probably tried to take the stuff yesterday but couldn't, so you came back today to pick it up."

31

"Are you trying to get me into trouble, Bart?" asked Greta.

"Maybe *you* did this, Bart," said Mortimer.

"Don't look at me," said Bart. "I didn't send anybody any messages. I don't even have a computer."

"Can you explain how your bookbag got here, Greta?" asked Officer Lawford. "If not, I'm afraid we've got a problem."

"I don't know how it got inside," said Greta. "All I know is I lost it yesterday after school."

"What are we going to do?" Mortimer whispered to Peter and Samantha. "Greta's really in trouble."

"I know how her bookbag got in the store," said Peter. "Bart put it there."

How does Peter know Bart is the culprit?

SOLUTION
The Case of the Mysterious E-Mail

"There are two clues," said Peter. "First, Bart, how did you know it was Greta's bookbag?"

"That's easy," said Bart. "I heard Officer Lawford say that."

"Maybe you did," said Peter. "But there's one thing you didn't know. And that's my second clue."

"What's that?" asked Bart.

"Greta's message," explained Peter. "She said she got a message telling her to come here, but she didn't say what kind."

"That's right," said Mortimer. "But Bart knew that the message was sent through E-mail."

"It could have been a phone message or a message on paper," said Samantha. "Bart knew because he sent it."

"His sister's in our class at school," Greta told Officer Lawford. "She must have told him we just started using E-mail in our computer class."

"Is that the way it is, Bart?" asked Officer Lawford.

"Yes," Bart admitted. "I don't want a girl helping me teach the class. I just wanted to get her in trouble with Mr. Lee. Then maybe he would kick her out of karate school."

"Well, Bart, here's a message for you," said Greta. "Now *you're* the one in trouble with Mr. Lee."

"Yeah," said Peter. "Let's see you karate kick your way out of this one."

4

The Case of the
Backwards Birthday

Greta was feeding her rabbits in her backyard when she heard her father calling her. "Greta, you got some mail." She ran to the back door, where Mr. Green handed her a brightly colored envelope. She quickly tore it open. It was a party invitation!

"It's from Bobby Blond," she told her father. "He's in my class at school."

"What kind of party is it?" Mr. Green asked.

"I don't know yet," said Greta, squinting at the invitation. "It's in code." On it Bobby had written, "Come to my SDRAWKCAB YADHTRIB YTRAP."

Greta ran inside to phone the other Clue Club kids. Sure enough, they had all received invitations. It didn't take them long to figure out that the message was written backwards. It said: "BACK-WARDS BIRTHDAY PARTY."

Next, Greta called Bobby to find out what they were going to do at his backwards party. Bobby explained that it was simple. "Everything is just done backwards," he told Greta. "Everyone has to wear their clothes backwards. And all our games will be played backwards. I couldn't think of a backwards kind of cake so we're going to have pineapple upside-down cake."

"What a cool idea," said Greta. "I can't wait for next Saturday."

When the kids arrived at Bobby's, they saw a sign on the front porch that read "ENTER THIS WAY." Below the sign was an arrow pointing to the back door.

"Of course," said Samantha. "At a backwards birthday party we should go into the house through the *back* door."

After all his guests were there, Bobby started the games. First he told everyone to go to the backyard, where they were going to have a race running backwards. The winner got a baseball cap that had to be worn backwards.

The kids jumped rope backwards, rode skateboards and scooters backwards, and shot baskets with their backs to the hoops. Peter was having so much fun that he decided he would walk everywhere backwards — until he almost knocked over the table with all of the presents on it.

For the last game, Bobby gave everyone an envelope with their name on the outside. Below each name was a strange word. Samantha's was spelled *Ahtnamas*. "What does this word mean?" she asked Bobby.

"That's how your name is spelled using my backwards code," answered Bobby.

Samantha looked at her friends' names. Peter was spelled *Retep,* Mortimer was *Remitrom,* and Greta was *Aterg.*

"Now, everyone, open your envelopes," Bobby told them.

Inside each envelope was a piece of paper with a coded message written on it. It read:

LLEPS SIHT EGASSEM SDRAWKCAB OT KCARC EHT EDOC DNA NIW A HSIFDLOG.

"What is the prize?" asked Mortimer.

"It's part of the message," said Bobby.

All the kids rushed to the table and began trying to figure out the code.

"Hmmm," Mortimer said to himself. "Hey! I think I know how to crack the code!" He started jotting down letters quickly.

After a few minutes, Mortimer suddenly jumped up. "I've got it!" he shouted.

"Wow! You're fast, Mortimer," said Peter.

"I love the prize, Bobby," said Mortimer.

"What is it, Mortimer?" asked Greta.

"My favorite pet!" he exclaimed.

How does Mortimer know what the coded message says? What is the prize?

SOLUTION
The Case of the Backwards Birthday

"The prize must be a goldfish," said Samantha. "That's Mortimer's favorite pet."

"That's right, Samantha," said Bobby.

"So what does the message say, Mortimer?" Peter asked.

"'Spell this message backwards to crack the code and win a goldfish,'" answered Mortimer, beaming. "It's like the code he used on his party invitations."

"I should have known that!" said Greta.

"Since everything at this party is backwards, does the goldfish swim backwards, too?" laughed Mortimer.

The Case of the Locker Mess

*B*rrrriiiiiinnnnnnng! rang the dismissal bell. Kids poured out of every classroom and headed for their lockers.

"Whew! Monday is finally over," said Mortimer.

"That social studies test was hard," Samantha said.

"Yeah," said Peter. "I hate tests on Monday. How'd you do, Greta?"

Greta didn't answer. She was busy trying to open her locker.

"Is your locker stuck again?" asked Peter.

"What else is new?" said Greta, shaking her head. She jiggled the lock, but it still wouldn't open.

"Want me to try?" asked Mortimer.

"That's okay," Greta said. "I'm just going

to get Mr. Gleamington. He can use his master key to open it for me." She walked off and returned moments later with the school janitor, who opened the locker for her.

"Thanks, Mr. Gleamington," said Greta.

"That's okay," the janitor answered. "I know these old lockers are hard to open. Well, at least they'll look better soon. They're going to be painted blue this weekend."

After Mr. Gleamington left, Peter opened his own locker. An avalanche of books, papers, and pencils tumbled out.

"Peter! Your locker is a total mess!" said Mortimer.

"That's why I'm putting this flag on it!" Peter said, laughing. He showed them a small flag that said *Peter's Mess* on it. The flag was on a metal rod that screwed onto a flat round disk at the bottom.

"That's the truth!" exclaimed Samantha. "What are you going to do with it?"

"Watch," Peter said. He unscrewed the rod and poked it through one of the small

holes in the locker door. Then he opened his locker and screwed the disk back onto the rod. "See?" he said. "Now the flag hangs out of my locker. The base keeps it from falling through the hole."

"Where'd you get that flag, anyway?" asked Samantha.

"My mom ordered it for me," Peter said. "She got it for my desk in my room, but I wanted to bring it to school."

Several other kids had gathered around Peter's locker while he was attaching his flag. "*Peter's Mess*," laughed one boy. "That's perfect, Peter."

"Hey! You need one of those flags, too, Pete," Greta said to Pete Pink. "Your locker looks as bad as Peter's."

Pete laughed. "No. Mine is worse," he said. "I think you should give me the flag, Peter. My mess deserves that flag more than yours."

"No way, Pete!" said Peter.

"Come on," said Pete. "I'll trade you something for the flag."

"If you really want one, you'll have to order one yourself," Peter told him. "You're not getting mine."

"Okay," said Pete. "Tell me where you got it."

Peter wrote down where his mother had ordered the flag. "Here, Pete, I hope you get one," he said. Then the kids collected their books and headed for home.

On Friday, when the kids went to their lockers after school, they saw that Peter's flag was gone. "Where's my flag?" Peter exclaimed.

"Wow! Someone must have broken it off," said Mortimer.

Peter opened the locker. "No," he said, after looking around inside for a moment. "The base is gone, too. If someone had broken off the flag, the base would have fallen to the bottom of the locker."

"Are you sure it's not there?" asked Mortimer.

"Yeah," said Greta. "How can you tell in all that mess?"

Samantha quickly looked through the locker. "Nope," she said. "It's gone, all right. Looks like we have a mystery."

"Let's have some pizza while we try to solve it," said Mortimer. The Clue kids headed for the pizza parlor. In between bites of pizza, they tried to figure out who had taken Peter's flag.

"I don't understand," said Peter. "How could anyone get inside my locker to take the flag?"

"There's another mystery," said Greta. "Why would anyone want a flag that says *Peter's Mess* on it?"

"Well, it has to be someone named Peter," said Mortimer. "Who else would want the flag?"

"There's Peter Plaid," said Samantha. "But he's very neat. I don't think he'd want a flag that said *mess* on it."

"Pete Pink!" said Mortimer. "Remember how much he liked your flag when you put it up?"

"Yeah," said Peter. "He tried to get me

to give it to him. Then he wanted to know where he could get one just like it."

"But we can't prove Pete took it," said Samantha.

"You can probably get another flag," Greta said.

"I know," said Peter. "But first I have to figure out how someone got the first one."

On Monday, when the kids returned to school, they saw that their lockers were painted blue. On Tuesday morning, Peter's flag was hanging from his locker again. "Look!" he called to his friends. "My flag is back."

"How did it get there?" asked Greta.

"Beats me," he said. "This mystery just keeps getting more and more mysterious."

"Wait a minute," said Mortimer, pointing to another locker. "Look."

Sticking out of a locker in another row was a flag that read *Pete's Pile*.

"Isn't that Pete Pink's locker?" said Greta.

"I think so," said Mortimer. "It looks like he got his own flag."

Bbbbrrriiinng! "There goes the warning bell," said Samantha. "We'd better get to class! Maybe we can figure this out at lunch."

The kids could hardly wait for lunchtime. When the bell finally rang, they were the first ones out of their seats.

"I thought lunch period would never come!" Peter told the others as they hurried to the lunchroom.

"Me, too," said Mortimer. "And not just because I'm hungry."

They grabbed four chairs at the end of a table and plopped down their lunch bags. Peter took a big swallow of his juice and asked, "So, what's going on with my flag?"

"It had to be Pete," said Mortimer, unwrapping a sandwich. "He must have taken it. Then he put it back when he got his own flag."

"But how did he get into my locker?" asked Peter.

"Does anyone have your locker key?" asked Greta.

"No," said Peter.

"Wait!" exclaimed Samantha, jumping up from the table. "I think I know who took your flag. It wasn't Pete Pink."

Who does Samantha think took Peter's flag? Why?

SOLUTION
The Case of the Locker Mess

"It was Mr. Gleamington," said Samantha.

"The janitor?" said Peter. "Why would he take it?"

"And then put it back?" added Greta.

"First, tell me something," said Samantha. "What color were our lockers on Friday?"

"Tan," said Peter.

"And what color are they today?" she asked.

"Blue," replied Mortimer. "A cool blue."

"They were painted over the weekend," said Greta.

"I get it!" said Peter. "Mr. Gleamington took my flag out so it wouldn't get messed up when he painted."

"And he used his master key to open your locker and put it back," said Greta.

"Let's ask him," said Samantha. She

pointed to the janitor, who was mopping up a spilled drink in the lunchroom. Sure enough, that's exactly what happened.

"I'm sorry, Peter. I forgot to tell you," the janitor explained.

"That's okay," said Peter. "Thanks to you, my mess flag isn't a mess like the rest of my locker."

The Case of the Doorbell Dodger

Dingdong! "Oh, hang on, Mortimer," cried Samantha. "There's the front doorbell again." She tossed the phone down on her bed, then ran down the stairs and threw open the front door. No one was there. "I knew it!" she shouted.

Samantha ran out into the yard and looked up and down the street. There was no one in sight. Then she ran to the back of the house. Still no one. "This is getting ridiculous!" she said.

She ran back up the stairs and picked up her phone. "Sorry about that," she told Mortimer. "Someone keeps ringing our doorbells, then running away. It's been going on for two weeks now."

"And you don't know who's doing it?" said Mortimer.

"Nope," she answered. "But it's really annoying. Sometimes they ring the front doorbell and sometimes the back. But we never can get to the door fast enough to catch whoever it is."

"How do you know which door to go to?" Mortimer asked.

"The front door sounds like chimes and the back door is a buzzer," said Samantha.

"Oh, yeah, I remember now," said Mortimer.

"When we first moved here, Dad said he couldn't tell the two bells apart," Samantha went on. "He was always going to the wrong door, so he put different sounds on each doorbell. Now we know if it's the front or back right away." She giggled. "The only problem is, the back doorbell is very quiet. Sometimes we don't hear it at all. But Dad won't fix it because we don't use the back door as much."

"Well, the Clue Club meeting is at your house this Saturday. Maybe the bell ringer will show up while we're there," Mortimer said.

"Yeah! Maybe we can catch him . . . or her!" exclaimed Samantha.

That Saturday, Samantha explained to the others about the mysterious bell ringer. "Why don't we have our meeting in the dining room instead of your room upstairs?" said Greta. "That way we'll be closer to both of the doors."

"Sounds good," said Samantha.

"This is exciting," said Peter. "Maybe we can solve a mystery during our Clue Jr. Club meeting."

"Well, let's call our meeting to order," said Mortimer.

The kids had finished their meeting and were just beginning their first game of Clue Jr. when they heard *Dingdong!*

"Aaaah!" cried Mortimer, startled.

"It's the front doorbell!" shouted Samantha. "Quick!"

They all jumped up and ran to the front

door. A boy was running across the yard. Samantha pulled the door open and the kids ran after him.

"Stop!" cried Peter. The boy turned around as the Clue Club surrounded him in the yard.

"What are you doing here?" Samantha said angrily.

"Uh, I'm selling raffle tickets for my school band," the boy replied.

"Why did you run away, then?" said Peter.

"I didn't run away. I just didn't think anyone was home," shrugged the boy. "No one answered the bell."

"You didn't give anybody a chance to!" said Samantha.

Just then Mr. Scarlet appeared at the door. "Can you come into the living room for a moment, son?" he asked the boy. "I have some questions I want to ask you about doorbells."

"Doorbells?" the boy said.

"Yes," said Mr. Scarlet. "Someone has

been ringing our doorbells, then running away. Just like you did today."

"I'm sorry if I caused any trouble," he said. "I didn't realize I left so quickly."

Inside, Mr. Scarlet asked the boy his name and address. The boy told them that his name was Damien Dull and he was a seventh grader who lived on the other side of town. He handed Mr. Scarlet some raffle tickets. "If you don't believe me, look at the raffle tickets," he said. "I've been all over town selling them."

Mr. Scarlet checked over the tickets. "Well, these *are* raffle tickets," he said. "We may owe you an apology, Damien."

"I told you that's what I was doing," said Damien. He got up to leave.

"I'd like you to wait here just a minute," said Mr. Scarlet. "I'm going to give your parents a call to see if they know you're this far from home."

Mr. Scarlet went to the kitchen and picked up the phone. He spoke to someone for a few minutes.

Buzzzzz! Buzzzzz! The back doorbell buzzed softly.

"What was that?" asked Greta, looking around.

"See, someone's at your back door now," Damien said. "Maybe it's the person who's been ringing your doorbells. That will prove it's not me."

Samantha ran to answer the back door. It was her next door neighbor, wanting to borrow a couple of eggs. After the neighbor left, Samantha returned to the living room. "It was just our neighbor," she told everyone.

At that Peter stood up and cleared his throat. "I know who the mystery bell ringer is," he announced.

"You do?" said Samantha.

Peter pointed to Damien. "It's you," he said.

How does Peter know Damien rang the doorbells?

"Well, this time I'll just give you a warning," Mr. Scarlet told Damien. "But if I catch you ringing our doorbells again, it will be something else."

"And I bet it won't be a door prize," laughed Mortimer.

SOLUTION
The Case of the Doorbell Dodger

"You can't prove that!" said Damien.

"Yes, I can," said Peter. "You told me yourself."

"What do you mean?" Damien said. "I told you I didn't do it."

"Peter's right," said Greta. "You told Samantha someone was at her back door."

"Yeah!" said Mortimer. "How did you know it was the back door?"

"There's only one way you could know that the back doorbell has a different sound than the front doorbell," said Peter.

"And that's if you rang both of them," exclaimed Samantha.

Damien admitted he had been ringing the doorbells.

"And I bet you carry the raffle tickets in case you get caught," said Mr. Scarlet. Damien nodded and promised he wouldn't do it again.

7

The Case of the Magazine Mix-up

One Friday, Ms. Redding gave her fourth-grade class an unusual reading assignment. "On Monday I'd like you to bring in a magazine that you enjoy reading outside of school," she told the students. "During the week we can all read them — including me! I think this will be a fun assignment."

"I know what magazine I'm bringing to school on Monday," Peter told the other Clue kids after school. He pulled a magazine out of his locker to show them. "*I Spy*, my favorite. But not the latest issue. I just got my copy in the mail and I'm not finished with it yet."

"I think I'll bring in *Fish Fan*," said Mortimer.

"*Fish Fan?*" said Greta. "You're probably the only person in the world who subscribes to that magazine."

"No, I'm not," said Mortimer. "Dottie Dun does. There *are* other people in the world who like fish, you know."

"What about you, Greta?" asked Peter.

"I guess I'll bring in *KIDS*," she said.

"What's that?" asked Mortimer.

"It stands for *Kids Into Doing Sports*," said Greta.

"I'm bringing in *Video View*," said Samantha.

"Oh, that's cool," said Peter. "I have a subscription to that, too."

"I love getting mail with my name on it," said Samantha.

"Me, too," said Mortimer.

"Ms. Redding is right. This *is* going to be a fun assignment," said Greta. "We get to read cool magazines all week."

On Monday, Ms. Redding cleared off the big table in the back of the room. "Please put your magazines on the table.

We'll spend our reading periods this week looking through them. On Friday you can take your magazines home."

The students gathered around the table to look at the magazines. "Look," Samantha whispered. "Six other kids brought in *Video View*. I knew it was popular."

"Wow!" exclaimed Mortimer. "So is *Fish Fan*. Check it out!" He pointed to two other issues lying on the table. "And they are both for this month," he said.

"Who brought them in?" asked Greta.

Mortimer peered at the mailing labels on the front of the magazines. Then he said, "One belongs to Millie Marble and the other is . . . I knew it! Dottie Dun."

All that week, the kids looked through the different magazines. On Wednesday at lunch, Mortimer told the kids that *Fish Fan* was getting some more fans. "Eddie Ebony asked if he could borrow mine after we were finished with it at school," he said proudly. "See, Greta? I told you other people like fish."

On Friday, Ms. Redding reminded the class to pick up their magazines after school. When the dismissal bell rang, everyone crowded around the table to get theirs.

"I'm going to my locker first," Mortimer said to his friends. "By the time I get my books, everyone will have cleared out, and it will be easier to find my magazine."

"That's a good idea," said Peter. So the four kids went to their lockers. As usual, Greta had trouble opening hers. By the time she had it open, most of the other fourth graders had found their magazines, gone to their lockers, and were heading out the school doors.

"See you Monday," Millie Marble hollered to Samantha as she slung her bookbag over her shoulder.

"Did you get your magazine yet?" Samantha asked.

"Yeah," Millie answered. "But it took a few minutes. It was pretty crowded around the table."

Greta finally had her books, so the kids

headed back to the classroom to collect their magazines. Dottie Dun was still looking through what was left.

"Do you see our magazines?" Mortimer asked her.

"Not yet," she said.

Mortimer spied one peeking from underneath another magazine. He picked it up and looked at the mailing label. "Here's yours," he said, handing Dottie the magazine.

"Here's mine," said Peter.

"Mine, too," said Greta.

"Mine three," giggled Samantha. "Now, where's yours, Mortimer?"

"I don't see it," Mortimer said. "Oh, I forgot. Eddie said he wanted to borrow it. He must have taken it. Let's go, or all the tables at the pizza parlor will be filled."

"That's right!" said Peter, as everyone hurried out the door.

At the pizza parlor, Mortimer spotted Eddie. "Did you get the *Fish Fan*?" Mortimer asked him.

"No," Eddie replied. "I couldn't find it. I figured you already took it."

"Hmmm," said Samantha. "I bet it's still there."

"Yeah," said Greta. "I guess we didn't look hard enough."

"Oh, well," said Mortimer, taking another bite of pizza. "I'll find it Monday. Meanwhile let's figure out what we're doing for our Clue Jr. Club meeting tomorrow morning."

The next Monday, when Mortimer walked into school, Ms. Redding met him at the classroom door. "The principal wants to see you in his office," she told him.

To Mortimer's surprise, Mr. Higgins said it looked like he had taken the new fish from the science room fish tank.

"Why do you think that?" asked Mortimer.

"Well, the science teacher discovered the fish were missing this morning. And she found your magazine beside the tank," explained Mr. Higgins. He held up a copy of

Fish Fan and pointed to the mailing label with Mortimer's name on it.

"Can you explain this, Mortimer?" Mr. Higgins asked.

"N-n-n-no," stuttered Mortimer. "I couldn't find my magazine on Friday, but I never went to the science room."

"I'm going to have to call your parents," said Mr. Higgins. "You'll have detention, of course. And I think you should pay for the fish, too."

At lunch, Mortimer was too upset to eat. "How did my magazine get in the science room?" he wondered.

"Maybe Eddie did take it after all," said Greta. "And he's lying about it."

"Yeah," said Peter. "Maybe he left it in the science room on purpose so you'd get blamed for taking the fish."

Suddenly Samantha hopped up from her chair. "No!" she exclaimed. "I know who took it!"

"You do?" asked Mortimer.

"Sure!" said Samantha. "It was Millie!"

"Millie?" said Mortimer.

"Yes," said Samantha, "and I can prove it."

How does Samantha know Millie took Mortimer's magazine?

SOLUTION
The Case of the Magazine Mix-up

"There were only three *Fish Fan* magazines on the table," said Samantha. "We saw Dottie take hers. And we know it was hers because we saw the mailing label."

"That's true," said Greta. "And Millie told us she took hers after school on Friday. So who took Mortimer's magazine?"

"Wait!" said Peter. "But Millie's magazine was still on the table. Remember? That's why we didn't take it. It had her name on it."

"Yes. So if Millie says she took one, that means she took Mortimer's," said Samantha.

"Of course," said Mortimer. "It's the only one she could take."

After lunch, the kids took Millie's *Fish Fan*, which was still on the table, and confronted her.

"Yeah, I took the fish," she admitted.

"But I didn't realize I left your magazine in the science room, Mortimer. I must have taken your magazine off the table by accident. I didn't know I got you into trouble."

"You'd better go tell Mr. Higgins," said Greta.

"Then Mortimer will be off the hook," said Samantha.

"Like a fish!" said Peter.

8

The Case of the Winning Skateboard

The weekly Clue Jr. Club meeting was at Peter's house. When the kids arrived, they found Peter in his garage.

"Brrrrr!" exclaimed Greta. "It's freezing!"

"What are you doing out here?" asked Mortimer.

"I'm oiling my skateboard wheels," Peter answered.

"What for?" asked Samantha. "You can't use your skateboard now. There's snow on the ground."

"Oh, I know," said Greta. "You're going to be in the indoor race at the rec center next Saturday."

"Yeah. The race was my idea," Peter said proudly. "Dad was trying to come up with some winter event the rec department could put on indoors. I told him I'd like to have a skateboard race on the indoor jogging track. He thought it was a great idea."

"That *is* a good idea," said Greta.

"Can anybody enter?" asked Samantha.

"Sure. There are different age groups," Peter answered. "My group is for fourth through sixth grades. The only thing is, I won't be able to practice if it keeps snowing."

"You don't need to," said Samantha. "You're probably the best skateboarder in the whole school."

"Thanks." Peter smiled. "I hope so."

"Maybe I'll enter, too," said Mortimer. "Think you could help me fix up my skateboard, Peter?"

"Sure, Mortimer," said Peter. "Do you have any oil? Or an Allen wrench?"

"Maybe some oil," said Mortimer. "What's an Allen wrench?"

Peter showed him a small L-shaped rod with a hexagonal end. "This is what you need to loosen and tighten the screws

74

that hold your wheels on," he told Mortimer. Peter turned his skateboard over to show Mortimer the wheels. "See?" he said. "The screws that hold the wheels on have six-sided holes in the tops. The Allen wrench has six sides, too, so it fits around the outside of the head of these screws."

"I see. Maybe you better bring that, too," said Mortimer. "Dad's not much on tools. But at least our garage is heated!"

When Peter finished oiling his skateboard; the kids went inside for their meeting. After a few games of Clue Jr. and some lunch, they headed over to Mortimer's.

Finally the day of the race arrived. Mortimer and Peter came early with Mr. Plum. They wanted to skateboard a little before the race and get loosened up.

"There's Brian Boysenberry," said Mortimer. He pointed to another fourth grader who was skating toward their group. "He's a really good skateboarder."

"Yeah, I know," said Peter. "That's why I

oiled my wheels so well." He twirled one of them and smiled while he watched it spin.

"Hey, guys," Katie Kolor called out. Katie was a sixth grader at their school. The boys waved at her. "Who do you think is going to win, Peter?" she asked.

"I hope I do," said Peter.

"Maybe Kasey will," Katie replied. She smiled and turned to her little brother. Kasey was also in the fourth grade. He was kneeling on the ground tightening his wheels. When he finished, he handed his sister a few small tools, which she slipped into her jeans pocket.

"Kasey and Brian are about the only kids in your group who might beat you," said Mortimer to Peter.

"Yeah, I know," said Peter. He looked up and waved. "Oh, here come Samantha and Greta."

"Hey, guys! Are you ready?" Greta called out.

"Well, I could use a hot dog," said Mortimer. "It will give me energy."

"Now?" said Peter. He shook his head and laughed. "Well, let's hurry." The boys leaned their skateboards against a wall, and the four kids hurried off to the hot dog stand.

Just as Mortimer was finishing his third hot dog, an announcement came over the loudspeakers. "Everyone in Group Four, please take your places at the starting line."

"That's us," said Peter. "Come on, Mortimer."

When the boys ran back to get their skateboards, they saw Brian leaning them up against the wall.

"What happened?" asked Peter.

"Your skateboards were on the ground," said Brian. "I was afraid someone would trip on them."

"Oh, thanks," said Mortimer. "Come on. Time to race!"

The three boys lined up with the other racers. *Tweeeeet!* went the whistle, and they all took off.

After going just a few yards, Peter felt his wheels start to wobble, so he stopped. He turned his skateboard over, then reached into his back pocket for his wrench. It wasn't there. Looking around, he saw Katie cheering for her brother Kasey.

"Katie, can I use your Allen wrench to tighten my wheels?" Peter called to her.

"I don't have one," said Katie. "Sorry."

Greta and Samantha came running up to Peter. "What's wrong?" cried Samantha.

"My wheels are loose," said Peter. "If I skate, they're going to fall off."

"Can't you tighten them?" asked Samantha.

"My Allen wrench is in my coat pocket," said Peter glumly. "It's back on the bench."

"Katie has one," said Greta. "Borrow hers."

"No, she doesn't," said Peter. "I asked her." Greta turned and ran back to Peter's coat. In a few minutes she returned holding the Allen wrench, but by the time Peter tightened his wheels, there was no way he could win. Kasey won, Brian came in second, and Mortimer came in fourth. Peter crossed the finish line in eleventh place.

"What happened?" Brian asked Peter afterwards. "How come you didn't start with us?"

"My wheels came loose," Peter told him.

"Too bad, Peter," said Kasey.

"Sorry I couldn't help you," Katie told Peter.

"I don't understand how this happened," said Peter, frowning. "I guess I didn't tighten the wheels enough when I oiled them."

"You tightened mine," said Mortimer, "and they were fine."

"I think someone loosened the wheels on your skateboard," said Greta.

"Who would do that?" cried Peter.

Mortimer turned to Brian. "Maybe you did," he said. "We caught you with our skateboards when we came back from the hot dog stand."

"I wouldn't do that!" said Brian. "I was just trying to move them out of the way."

"No! No! It wasn't Brian," said Greta.

"Then who loosened Peter's wheels?" asked Samantha.

"Big sister," Greta said, turning to Katie.

"Me?" cried Katie. "Why me?"

"To help Kasey win," Greta said.

"You can't prove that," said Katie.

"I think I can," said Greta.

Why does Greta think Katie loosened Peter's wheels?

"That's why our skateboards weren't up against the wall where we left them," Peter said.

"Greta's right," Katie said. "I didn't think Kasey could win if you were in the race. Sorry, Peter."

"Well, I don't want to win this way," said Kasey. "Let's tell your dad, Peter. Maybe we can do the race again."

"After Peter tightens his wheels, this race will be tighter, too," said Mortimer.

SOLUTION
The Case of the Winning Skateboard

"How come you told Peter you didn't have an Allen wrench?" Greta asked Katie. "I saw you put one in your jeans pocket just before the race."

Katie pulled the wrench out of her pocket. "Oh, is this an Allen wrench? I didn't know what kind I had."

"Then how did you know you didn't have it?" said Greta. "Besides, I saw Kasey using it to tighten his wheels. Then he gave it to you and you put it in your jeans pocket."

"You had to know that wrench could tighten Peter's wheels if it tightened Kasey's," said Samantha. "You just didn't want to help Peter!"

"Especially after you loosened his wheels while he was getting a hot dog with me," said Mortimer.